For pattern inquiries, please visit: www.go-crafty.com

Gifty Wristers

MATERIALS

Yarn

RED HEART *Heart & Sole*,
1¾oz/50g balls, each approx
213yd/195m (superwash
wool/nylon)
• 2 balls #3966 Toasted Almond

Hook

• Size D/3 (3.25mm) crochet hook
or size to obtain gauge

Notions

• 4 buttons— ⅜"/9mm diameter
• Stitch markers
• Yarn needle

FINISHED MEASUREMENTS

Length Approx 8"/20.5cm
Circumference Approx 9"/23cm at
widest point

GAUGE

24 sts and 30 rows = 4"/10cm over pattern
stitch (alternating sl st and hdc)
Take time to check gauge.

NOTES

1 Leave long tails when fastening off near
fingers. Use tails to close any small
holes between fingers.
2 Take care when working the alternating
half double crochet and slip stitch
pattern. The thin, variegated yarn can
make the slip stitches a bit difficult to
see. Take care to work slip stitches
loosely, and count the number of
stitches in each row or round.
3 The buttons and button loops were
intended to be worn on the inside of the
wrist, but you may prefer the buttons on
the outside.

GLOVE (MAKE 2)

Beginning at Cuff, ch 39.
Row 1 (right side) Sl st in 2nd ch from
hook, hdc in next ch, *sl st in next ch, hdc
in next ch; repeat from * across—38 sts.
Rows 2–10 Ch 1, turn; *sl st in next hdc,
hdc in next sl st; repeat from * across.
Row 11 Ch 7, turn; sl st in 2nd ch from
hook and in next 5 chs (button loop
started), *sl st in next hdc, hdc in next sl
st; repeat from * across.
Row 12 Repeat Row 2. Do not work any
sts into button loop at end of row. Place a
marker at beginning of this row for button
placement.
Row 13 Ch 1, turn; inserting hook through
tip of button loop and into first hdc, work a
sl st (button loop completed), hdc in next
sl st, *sl st in next hdc, hdc in next sl st;
repeat from * across.
Row 14 Repeat Row 2.
Rows 15–17 Repeat Rows 11–13. Place a
marker at beginning of Row 16 for button
placement.
Rows 18–22 Repeat Row 2, 5 more times.
Place markers in 9th and 30th st on Row 22.
Note When you reach a marker, remove
marker, work stitch(es) into marked stitch
as instructed, then replace marker in stitch
indicated or in stitch worked.
Row 23 Ch 1, turn; *sl st in next hdc, hdc
in next sl st; repeat from * across to next
marker, (sl st, hdc, sl st) in marked st,
move marker to last sl st made, **hdc in
next sl st, sl st in next hdc; repeat from **
across to next marker, (hdc, sl st, hdc) in
marked st, move marker to 2nd to last hdc
made, ***sl st in next hdc, hdc in next sl
st; repeat from *** across—42 sts.
Row 24 Ch 1, turn; (sl st, hdc, sl st) in next
hdc, *hdc in next sl st, sl st in next hdc;
repeat from * across to last sl st, (hdc, sl
st, hdc) in last sl st—46 sts.
Row 25 Repeat Row 23—50 sts. Remove
markers.

Join to Work in the Round

Round 26 Repeat Row 24; join with sl st
in first sl st—54 sts.
Round 27 Ch 1, turn; *sl st in next hdc,

hdc in next sl st; repeat from * around; join
with sl st in first sl st.
Repeat Round 27 until piece measures
about 5½"/14cm from beginning, ending by
working a wrong side row.

Divide for Thumb

Round 1 (right side) Ch 1, turn; [sl st in
next hdc, hdc in next sl st] 5 times, ch 3
(thumb dividing chain), sk next 13 sts, hdc
in next sl st, *sl st in next hdc, hdc in next
sl st; repeat from * around; join with sl st
in first sl st—44 sts (including 3 chs).
Round 2 Ch 1, turn; [sl st in next hdc, hdc
in next sl st] 15 times, sl st in next hdc,
hdc in next ch, sl st in next ch, hdc in next
ch, [sl st in next hdc, hdc in next sl st] 5
times; join with sl st in first sl st.
Round 3 Ch 1, turn; *sl st in next hdc, hdc
in next sl st; repeat from * around; join
with sl st in first sl st.
Repeat Round 3 until piece measures
approximately 1¼"/3cm from beginning of
thumb divide, ending by working a wrong
side row.

Divide for Pinky

Round 1 (right side) Ch 1, turn; [sl st in
next hdc, hdc in next sl st] 14 times, sl st
in next hdc, ch 2 (pinky dividing chain), sk
next 10 sts, hdc in next sl st, [sl st in next
hdc, hdc in next sl st] 2 times; join with sl
st in first sl st—36 sts (including 2 chs).
Round 2 Ch 1, turn; [sl st in next hdc, hdc
in next sl st] 2 times, sl st in next hdc, hdc
in next ch, sl st in next ch, hdc in next sl
st, [sl st in next hdc, hdc in next sl st] 14
times; join with sl st in first sl st.
Rounds 3 and 4 Ch 1, turn; *sl st in
next hdc, hdc in next sl st; repeat from *
around; join with sl st in first sl st.

Divide for Ring, Middle, and Index Fingers

Round 1 (right side) Ch 1, turn; [sl st in
next hdc, hdc in next sl st] 3 times, ch 2
(index finger dividing chain), sk next 12 sts,
[sl st in next hdc, hdc in next sl st] 3 times,
ch 2 (ring finger dividing chain), sk next
12 sts; join with sl st in first sl st—16 sts
(including 4 chs).

Gifty Wristers

Complete Middle Finger

Round 2 Ch 1, turn; *sl st in next ch, hdc in next ch, [sl st in next hdc, hdc in next sl st] 3 times; repeat from * once more; join with sl st in first sl st.

Rounds 3–7 Ch 1, turn; *sl st in next hdc, hdc in next sl st; repeat from * around; join with sl st in first sl st.
Fasten off.

Complete Thumb

With right side facing, join yarn with sl st in first skipped hdc after thumb dividing chain.

Round 1 Working in all sts and free loops along opposite side of dividing chain, hdc in next st, *sl st in next st, hdc in next st; repeat from * around; join with sl st in first sl st—16 sts.

Rounds 2–5 Ch 1, turn; *sl st in next hdc, hdc in next sl st; repeat from * around; join with sl st in first sl st.
Fasten off.

Complete Pinky, Ring, and Index Fingers

With right side facing, join yarn with sl st in first skipped hdc after dividing chain on Pinky, Ring, or Index Finger.

Rounds 1–5 Work same as Rounds 1–5 on Thumb—12 sts on Pinky, 14 sts on Ring and Index Fingers.
Fasten off.
Repeat for other 2 fingers.

FINISHING

Turn one glove inside out (for other hand). On each glove, sew two buttons on marked rows, opposite button loops.
Weave in ends. ∎

Snowflake Scarf

MATERIALS

Yarn  ❨4❩

RED HEART *Soft*, 5oz/140g skeins, each approx 256yd/234m (acrylic)
• 3 skeins #4604 Navy

Hook
• Size H/8 (5mm) crochet hook *or size to obtain gauge*

Notions
• Yarn needle
• Straight pins for blocking
• Spray bottle of water

STITCH GLOSSARY

Picot Ch 3, sl st in 3rd ch from hook.
Beginning X-St (beginning crossed stitch) Ch 3, sk next 2 dc, dc in next dc, ch 6, dc in top of last dc made.
X-st (crossed stitch) Yo 3 times, insert hook in first dc, yo and draw up a lp, [yo and draw through 2 lps on hook] twice (2 lps rem on hook); sk next 2 dc, dc in next dc, [yo and draw through 2 lps on hook] twice; ch 3, dc in top of dc just made.
Beginning cl (beginning cluster) Ch 2, [yo, insert hook in specified st or sp, yo and draw up a lp, yo and draw through 2 lps on hook] 2 times; yo and draw through all 3 lps on hook.
Cl (cluster) [Yo, insert hook in specified st or sp, yo and draw up a lp, yo and draw through 2 lps on hook] 3 times; yo and draw through all 4 lps on hook.
Ch-3 join Ch 1, sl st in corresponding ch-3 sp on round/row 4 of adjacent motif, ch 1.
Ch-5 join Ch 2, sl st in corresponding ch-5 sp on round/row 4 of adjacent motif, ch 2.
Picot join Ch 1, sl st in ch-3 sp of picot on round/row 4 of adjacent motif, ch 1, sl st in first ch.

FINISHED MEASUREMENTS
Length Approx 60"/152.5cm
Width Approx 10½"/26.5cm

GAUGE
Snowflake Motif = 6¼"/16cm diameter between ch-5 sps
Rounds 1 and 2 of snowflake motif = 3"/7.5cm diameter between picots
Take time to check gauge.

NOTES
1 Join opposite edges of Snowflake Motifs into a long strip of 9 motifs.
2 Make sure all motifs are right side facing before joining.
3 Join End Snowflake Motifs to each end of Snowflake Motif strip.
4 Make sure all motifs are right side facing before joining.
5 Side Snowflake Motifs are always joined to 2 unjoined edges of 2 Snowflake Motifs or 1 Snowflake Motif and 1 End Snowflake Motif. They are not always joined to an adjacent Side Snowflake Motif.
6 Whenever joining Side Snowflake Motif to an adjacent motif, work "picot join" or "ch-3 join" at beginning or end of row 4. When there is not an adjacent motif for joining, simply work "picot" or "ch 3."
7 When there are already 2 adjacent joined motifs, work sl st of "ch-5 join" in each adjacent joined ch-5 sp.
8 Make sure all motifs are right side facing before joining.

SCARF

First Snowflake Motif
Ch 6, join with sl st to form a ring.
Round 1 (right side) Ch 3 (counts as dc now and throughout), dc in ring, ch 3, [2 dc in ring, ch 3] 5 times—12 dc and 6 ch-3 sps. Join with sl st in 3rd ch of beginning ch-3.
Round 2 Ch 3, dc in same ch as joining, 2 dc in next dc, ch 1, picot, ch 1, sk next ch-3 sp, [2 dc in each of next 2 dc, ch 1, picot, ch 1, sk next ch-3 sp] 5 times—24 dc and 6 picots. Join with sl st in 3rd ch of beginning ch-3.
Round 3 Work beginning X-st, ch 3, picot, ch 3, sk next picot, [work X-st over next 4 dc, ch 3, picot, ch 3, sk next picot] 5 times—6 X-sts and 6 picots. Join with sl st in 3rd ch of ch-6 sp on beginning X-st.
Round 4 Work (beginning cl, ch 3, cl, ch 5, cl, ch 3, cl) in ch-3 sp of beginning X-st, ch 3, picot, ch 3, sk next picot, [(cl, ch 3, cl, ch 5, cl, ch 3, cl) in ch-3 sp of next X-st, ch 3, picot, ch 3, sk next picot] 5 times—24 cl and 6 picots. Join with sl st in top of beginning cl. Fasten off.

Second–Ninth Snowflake Motifs
Ch 6, join with sl st to form a ring.
Rounds 1–3 Work same as Rounds 1–3 on First Snowflake Motif.
Round 4 (joining round) Work (beginning cl, ch 3, cl, ch 5, cl, ch 3, cl) in ch-3 sp of beginning X-st, ch 3, picot, ch 3, sk next picot, [(cl, ch 3, cl, ch 5, cl, ch 3, cl) in ch-3 sp of next X-st, ch 3, picot, ch 3, sk next picot] 3 times; *(cl, ch 3, cl, ch-5 join, cl, ch-3 join, cl) in ch-3 sp of next X-st; ch 3, picot join, ch 3, sk next picot; (cl, ch-3 join,

cl, ch-5 join, cl, ch 3, cl) in ch-3 sp of next X-st; ch 3, picot, ch 3, sk next picot*—24 cl and 6 picots. Join with sl st in top of beginning cl. Fasten off.

End Snowflake Motif (make 2)

Ch 6, join with sl st to form a ring.

Row 1 (wrong side) Ch 6 (counts as dc and ch-3 sp), [2 dc in ring, ch 3] twice, dc in ring—6 dc and 3 ch-3 sps. Turn.

Row 2 Ch 3 (counts as dc), dc in first dc, ch 1, picot, ch 1, sk next ch-3 sp, [2 dc in each of next 2 dc, ch 1, picot, ch 1, sk next ch-3 sp] 2 times; 2 dc in 3rd ch of beginning ch-3—12 dc and 3 picots. Turn.

Row 3 Ch 3, dc in next dc, ch 6, dc in top of last dc made (beginning X-st made), ch 3, picot, ch 3, [sk next picot, X-st over next 4 dc, ch 3, picot, ch 3] 2 times; sk next picot, X-st over last 2 dc—4 X-sts and 3 picots. Turn.

Row 4 (joining round) Ch 6 (counts as beginning ch-5 sp), (cl, ch 3, cl) in ch-3 sp of first X-st, ch 3, picot, ch 3, sk next picot; repeat from [to] on Round 4 of Second–Ninth Snowflake Motifs; (cl, ch 3, cl) in ch-6 sp of beginning X-st, ch 6 (counts as ending ch-5 sp)—12 cl and 3 picots. Join with sl st in 3rd ch of same ch-6 sp on beginning X-st. Fasten off.

SIDE SNOWFLAKE MOTIF (MAKE 20)

Ch 6, join with sl st to form a ring.

Row 1 (wrong side) Ch 5 (counts as tr and ch-1 sp), [2 dc in ring, ch 3] twice, (2 dc, ch 1, tr) in ring—2 tr, 6 dc, 2 ch-3 sps and 2 ch-1 sps. Turn.

Row 2 Ch 5, [2 dc in each of next 2 dc, ch 1, picot, ch 1, sk next ch-3 sp] twice; 2 dc in each of next 2 dc, ch 1, tr in 4th ch of beginning ch-5—2 tr, 12 dc, 2 picots and 2 ch-1 sps. Turn.

Row 3 Ch 7 (counts as tr and ch-3 sp), sk next ch-sp or picot, [X-st over next 4 dc, ch 3, picot, ch 3, sk next ch-sp] 2 times; X-st over next 4 dc, ch 3, tr in 4th ch of beginning ch-5—2 tr, 3 X-sts, 2 picots and 6 ch-3 sps. Turn.

Row 4 (joining round) Ch 3, picot or picot join, ch 3, sk next ch-sp, *(cl, ch 3 or ch-3 join, cl, ch-5 join, cl, ch 3 or ch-3 join, cl) in ch-3 sp of next X-st**; ch 3, picot join,

ch 3, sk next picot; repeat from * once; repeat from * to ** once; ch 3, picot or picot join, ch 3—12 cl and 4 picots. Join with sl st in 4th ch of beginning ch-7. Fasten off.

BLOCKING

Lay joined motifs on a flat surface such as a blocking board or towels. Pin to schematic size, spritz with water and allow to dry before continuing.

Edging

With right side facing, join with sl st in any sp around edge, ch 1, sc in same sp as joining, sc evenly spaced along all edges around entire scarf. Join with sl st in first sc. Fasten off.

FINISHING

Weave in all ends. ■

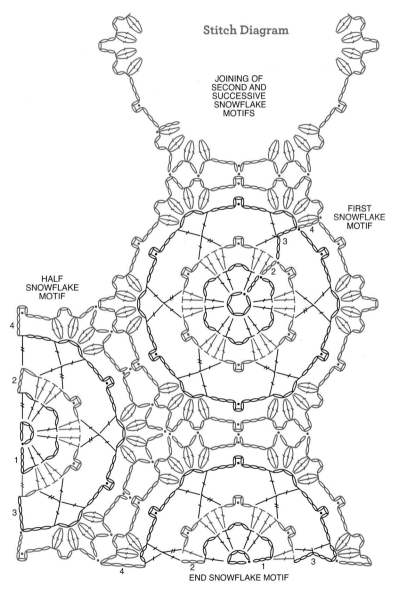

Stitch Diagram

JOINING OF SECOND AND SUCCESSIVE SNOWFLAKE MOTIFS

FIRST SNOWFLAKE MOTIF

HALF SNOWFLAKE MOTIF

END SNOWFLAKE MOTIF

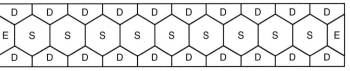

D	D	D	D	D	D	D	D	D	D	D
E	S	S	S	S	S	S	S	S	S	E
D	D	D	D	D	D	D	D	D	D	D

CONSTRUCTION DIAGRAM

CHART KEY
S = Snowflake
D = Side snowflake
E = End snowflake

Snowflake Wristlets

MATERIALS

Yarn 1

RED HEART *Heart & Sole*, 1¾oz/50g balls, each approx 213yd/195m (superwash wool/nylon)
• 1 ball #3115 Ivory

Hook

• Size C/2 (2.75mm) crochet hook *or size to obtain gauge*

Notions

• Yarn needle

STITCH GLOSSARY

2-dc Cl (2 double crochet cluster) Yarn over, insert hook in indicated st or sp, yarn over and draw up a loop, yarn over and draw through 2 loops on hook; yarn over, insert hook in same st or sp, yarn over and draw up a loop, yarn over and draw through 2 loops on hook, yarn over and draw through all 3 loops on hook.

3-dc Cl (3 double crochet cluster) Yarn over, insert hook in indicated st or sp, yarn over and draw up a loop, yarn over and draw through 2 loops on hook; [yarn over, insert hook in same st or sp, yarn over and draw up a loop, yarn over and draw through 2 loops on hook] twice, yarn over and draw through all 4 loops on hook.

ch-5 sp join Ch 2, sl st in neighboring ch-5 sp, ch 2.

ch-7 sp join Ch 3, sl st in neighboring ch-7 sp, ch 3.

FINISHED MEASUREMENTS

Circumference Approx 6¾"/17cm
Note Fabric is stretchy and will fit larger circumference wrists. To make larger wristlets, use a larger hook. A hook one size larger will yield a wristlet approx 7½"/19cm circumference. A hook two sizes larger will yield a wristlet approx 8¼"/21cm circumference.

GAUGE

1 Motif = 2¼" x 2¼"/5.5cm x 5.5cm.
Take time to check gauge.

FIRST MOTIF

Ch 5; join with sl st in first ch to form a ring.
Round 1 Ch 4 (counts as first dc, ch 1), [dc in ring, ch 1] 11 times; join with sl st in 3rd ch of beginning ch—12 dc and 12 ch-1 sps.
Round 2 Ch 3 (counts as first dc), 2-dc Cl in first ch-1 sp, ch 5, [3-dc Cl in next ch-1 sp, ch 5] 11 times; join with sl st in first Cl—12 clusters and 12 ch-5 sps.
Round 3 Sl st in first ch-5 sp, ch 1, (sc, ch 7, sc) in same ch-5 sp (corner made), *[ch 5, sc in next ch-5 sp] twice, ch 5, (sc, ch 7, sc) in next ch-5 sp (corner made); repeat from * 2 more times, [ch 5, sc in next ch-5 sp] twice, ch 5; join with sl st in first sc—4 ch-7 corners and 3 ch-5 sps along each side. Fasten off.

SECOND–SIXTH MOTIF

Work as for first motif through Round 2. Refer to assembly diagram for placement of motif. Refer to definitions of ch-7 sp join and ch-5 sp join as you work Round 3 (joining round). If a ch-7 or ch-5 has a corresponding ch-sp on a neighboring motif, work a ch-7 sp join or ch-5 sp join instead of the ch-7 or ch-5; Sl st in first ch-5 sp, ch 1, (sc, ch 7, sc) in same ch-5 sp (corner made), *[ch 5, sc in next ch-5 sp] twice, ch 5, (sc, ch 7, sc) in next ch-5 sp (corner made); repeat from * 2 more times, [ch 5, sc in next ch-5 sp] twice, ch 5; join with sl st in first sc—4 ch-7 corners and 3 ch-5 sps along each side. Fasten off.
You should now have a ring of motifs, 2 motifs wide and 3 motifs in circumference.

FINISHING

Edging
Join yarn with sl st in any corner ch-7 sp along edge of wristlet; ch 1, sc in same ch-7 sp, ch 5, *sc in next ch-sp, ch 5; repeat from * around; join with sl st in first sc. Fasten off. Repeat around other wristlet edge.
Weave in all ends. ■

Stitch Diagram

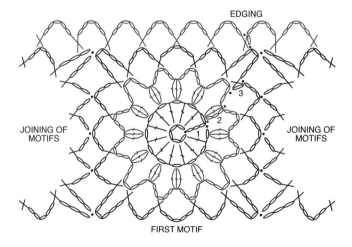

JOINING OF MOTIFS

JOINING OF MOTIFS

EDGING

FIRST MOTIF

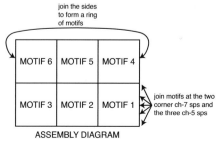

join the sides to form a ring of motifs

| MOTIF 6 | MOTIF 5 | MOTIF 4 |
| MOTIF 3 | MOTIF 2 | MOTIF 1 |

join motifs at the two corner ch-7 sps and the three ch-5 sps

ASSEMBLY DIAGRAM

Men's Two-Hour Hat

Rose Callahan

FINISHED MEASUREMENTS
Circumference Approx 21"/53.5cm; stretches to fit most men's heads

GAUGE
14 sc and 15 rows worked in back loop = 4"/10cm square
Take time to check gauge.

HAT
Ch 32, leaving an 18"/45.5cm tail for sewing.

Row 1 (wrong side) Sc in 2nd ch from hook and in each remaining ch across—31 sc.

Row 2 Ch 1, turn; working in back loops, sc in first 30 sc, leaving last sc unworked—30 sc.

Row 3 Ch 1, turn; working in back loops, sc in each sc across—30 sc.

Row 4 Ch 1, turn; working in back loops, sc in each sc across, sc in unworked sc 3 rows below—31 sc.

Row 5 Repeat Row 3—31 sc.

Rows 6–72 Repeat Rows 2–5, 16 more times, then repeat Rows 2–4 once more. At end of last row, fasten off, leaving an 18"/45.5cm tail for sewing.

FINISHING
With right sides together, thread tail in and out of each hole created by unworked sc and pull taut to gather top of hat. Secure tail. Whipstitch first and last rows together to form side seam. Weave in ends. Turn right side out. ∎

Fingerless Gloves

Paul Amato for Lvarepresents.com

MATERIALS

Yarn (3)

RED HEART *Bella*, 3½oz/100g balls, each approx 328yd/300m (acrylic)
• 1 ball #01001 Marble Color

Hook

• Size D/3 (3.25mm) crochet hook *or size to obtain gauge*

Notions

• 2 belt clasps ¾"/2cm diameter
• Stitch markers
• Yarn needle

STITCH GLOSSARY

FPdtr (front post double treble crochet) Yarn over 3 times, insert hook from front to back to front around indicated st, yarn over and draw a loop, [yarn over and draw up through 2 loops on hook] 4 times.
Note Do not skip the st behind FPdtr.

FINISHED MEASUREMENTS

Approx 7"/18cm around palm, excluding thumb.

GAUGE

18 hdc and 15 rows = 4"/10 cm using size D/3 (3.25mm) crochet hook.
Take time to check gauge.

GLOVE (MAKE 2)

Beginning at wrist, ch 34.
Row 1 Hdc in 3rd ch from hook and each ch across—32 hdc.
Rows 2 and 3 Ch 2 (does not count as st here and throughout), turn, hdc in each hdc across.
Row 4 (strap loop row) Ch 2, turn, hdc in first 3 hdc, FPdtr around 3rd hdc 3 rows below, *hdc in next 3 hdc, sk 2 hdc 3 rows below, FPdtr around next hdc 3

rows below; repeat from * 8 times, hdc in last 2 hdc—10 FPdtr.
Row 5 Ch 2, turn, hdc in each hdc across to first FPdtr, *sk FPdtr, hdc in each hdc across to next FPdtr; repeat from * across—32 hdc.
Note Ends of work will be joined and work will proceed in rounds.
Rnds 6–8 Ch 2, turn, hdc in each hdc across; join with sl st in top of beginning ch-2.
Rnd 9 Ch 2, turn, hdc in next 14 hdc, 2 hdc in next hdc, hdc in next 2 hdc, 2 hdc in next hdc, hdc in last 14 hdc; join with sl st in top of beginning ch-2—34 hdc.
Rnd 10 Ch 2, turn, hdc in next 15 hdc, 2 hdc in next hdc, hdc in next 2 hdc, 2 hdc in next hdc, hdc in last 15 hdc; join with sl st in top of beginning ch-2—36 hdc.
Rnd 11 Ch 2, turn, hdc in next 16 hdc, 2 hdc in next hdc, hdc in next 2 hdc, 2 hdc in next hdc, hdc in last 16 hdc; join with sl st in top of beginning ch-2—38 hdc.
Rnd 12 Ch 2, turn, hdc in next 17 hdc, 2 hdc in next hdc, hdc in next 2 hdc, 2 hdc in next hdc, hdc in last 17 hdc; join with sl st in top of beginning ch-2—40 hdc.
Rnd 13 Ch 2, turn, hdc in next 18 hdc, 2 hdc in next hdc, hdc in next 2 hdc, 2 hdc in next hdc, hdc in last 18 hdc; join with sl st in top of beginning ch-2—42 hdc.
Rnds 14 and 15 Ch 2, turn, hdc in each st across; join with sl st in top of beginning ch-2.
Rnd 16 Ch 2, turn, hdc in next 16 hdc, place marker in hdc just made, hdc in next 11 hdc, sl st in marked hdc to form thumb, hdc in next 15 hdc; join with sl st in top of beginning ch-2—30 palm hdc and 12 thumb hdc.
Rnd 17 Ch 2, turn, hdc in 30 hdc of palm, skip thumb hdc; join with sl st in top of beginning ch-2.

Rnds 18 and 19 Ch 2, turn, hdc in each hdc around; join with sl st in top of beginning ch-2.
Rnd 20 Ch 2, hdc in next 12 hdc, place markers in 4th, 8th and 12th hdc just made, hdc in next 7 hdc, sc in marked 12th hdc to form index finger, hdc in next 4 hdc, sc in marked 8th hdc to form middle finger, hdc in next 4 hdc, sc in marked 4th hdc to form ring finger, hdc in next 3 hdc; join with sl st in top of beginning ch. Fasten off.

STRAPS (MAKE 2)

Work 2 sl sts around belt clasp.
Row 1 Ch 2, turn, hdc in each st across—2 hdc.
Repeat Row 1 until strap measures 10"/25.5cm. Fasten off. Thread strap through belt loops and fasten into clasp.

FINISHING

Weave in all ends. ■

Lumberjack Hat

MATERIALS

Yarn [4] [6]

RED HEART *Super Saver*,
7oz/198g skeins, each approx
364yd/333m (acrylic)
• 1 skein #0360 Café Latte (A)
RED HEART *Light & Lofty*,
6oz/170g skeins, each approx
140yd/128m (acrylic)
• 1 skein #9334 Café au Lait (B)

Hook
• Size K/10½(6.5mm) crochet
  hook *or size to obtain gauge*

Notions
• Stitch marker
• Yarn needle

STITCH GLOSSARY

Sc2tog (sc 2 stitches together) [Insert
hook in next st, yarn over and draw
up a loop] 2 times, yarn over and draw
through all 3 loops on hook.

FINISHED MEASUREMENTS

Small Approx 20"/51cm circumference
Large Approx 22"/56cm circumference

GAUGE

Exterior Rounds 1–5 = 4"/10cm diameter.
Take time to check gauge.

NOTE

Body of hat is worked in the round as a
spiral. Front flap, back flap and earflaps are
worked in rows.

EXTERIOR HAT BODY
(SMALL SIZE)

Starting at crown, with 2 strands of A, ch 2.

Round 1 (right side) Work 8 sc in 2nd ch
from hook—8 sc. Place marker in first sc
and move up to first sc in each round to
mark beginning of rounds.
Round 2 Work 2 sc in each st around—16
sc.
Round 3 [Sc in next st, 2 sc in next st] 8
times—24 sc.
Round 4 [Sc in next 2 sts, 2 sc in next st]
8 times—32 sc.
Round 5 [Sc in next 3 sts, 2 sc in next st]
8 times—40 sc.
Round 6 Sc in each st around.
Round 7 [Sc in next 4 sts, 2 sc in next st]
8 times—48 sc.
Round 8 Repeat Round 6.
Round 9 [Sc in next 23 sts, 2 sc in next st]
2 times—50 sc.
Rounds 10–17 Repeat Round 6, 8 times
more. Do not fasten off.

FRONT FLAP

Row 1 Working in front loops only, sc in next
15 sts, leaving rem sts unworked—15 sc.
Rows 2–5 Ch 1, turn; sc in each st across.
Row 6 Ch 1, turn; sc2tog, sc in next 11
sts, sc2tog—13 sc.
Row 7 Ch 1, turn; sc2tog, sc in next 9 sts,
sc2tog—11 sc.
Row 8 Repeat Row 2. Fasten off.

EXTERIOR HAT BODY
(LARGE SIZE)

Starting at crown, with 2 strands of A, ch 2.
Rounds 1–8 Work same as Rounds 1–8 of
size small Exterior Hat Body.
Round 9 [Sc in next 11 sts, 2 sc in next st]
4 times—52 sc.
Round 10 Repeat Round 6.
Round 11 [Sc in next 12 sts, 2 sc in next
st] 4 times—56 sc.
Rounds 12–19 Repeat Round 6, 8 times
more. Do not fasten off.

FRONT FLAP

Row 1 Working in front loops only,
sc in next 18 sts, leaving rem sts
unworked—18 sc.
Rows 2–6 Ch 1, turn; sc in each st across.

Row 7 Ch 1, turn; sc2tog, sc in next 14
sts, sc2tog—16 sc.
Row 8 Ch 1, turn; sc2tog, sc in next 12
sts, sc2tog—14 sc.
Row 9 Repeat Row 2. Fasten off.

BACK FLAP (BOTH SIZES)

Row 1 With right side facing and top of
hat facing downward, skip next st on last
round of Exterior Hat Body after last st
worked on row 1 of Front Flap, working in
front loops only, join 2 strands of A with sl
st in next st, ch 1, sc in same st as joining
and in next 32 (35) sts, leaving last st
unworked—33 (36) sc.
Rows 2–5 (7) Ch 1, turn; sc in each st
across. Do not fasten off.

RIGHT EARFLAP (BOTH SIZES)

Row 1 (wrong side) Ch 1, turn; sc in first
8 (10) sc, leaving rem sts unworked—8
(10) sc.
Rows 2–6 (7) Ch 1, turn; sc in each st
across.
Row 7 (8) Ch 1, turn; sc2tog, sc in next 4
(6) sts, sc2tog—6 (8) sc.
Row 8 (9) Ch 1, turn; sc2tog, sc in next 2
(4) sts, sc2tog—4 (6) sc.
Row 9 (10) Ch 1, turn; sc in first 2 (3) sts,
ch 31, sl st in 2nd ch from hook and in
each rem ch across (tie made), sc in last 2
(3) sc—4 (6) sc and 1 tie. Fasten off.

LEFT EARFLAP (BOTH SIZES)

Row 1 With wrong side facing and top
of hat facing downward, sk next 17 (16)
sts on last row of Back Flap after last st
worked on Row 1 of Right Earflap, join
2 strands of A with sl st in next st, ch 1,
sc in same st as joining and in next 7 (9)
sts—8 (10) sc.
Rows 2–9 (10) Work same as Rows 2–9
(10) on Right earflap.

INTERIOR FUR LINING
FRONT FLAP (BOTH SIZES)

Row 1 Fold Exterior Front Flap to right
side. With right side facing and top of hat
facing downward, working in back loops

Lumberjack Hat

only of same sts as Row 1 of Exterior Front Flap, join B with sl st in first st behind Exterior Front Flap, ch 1, sc in same st as joining and in next 14 (17) sts—15 (18) sc.

Rows 2–8 (9) Work same as Rows 2–8 (9) of Exterior Front Flap.

BACK FLAP (BOTH SIZES)

Row 1 Fold Exterior Back Flap to right side. With right side facing and top of hat facing downward, working in back loops only of same sts as Row 1 of Exterior Back Flap, join B with sl st in first st behind Exterior Back Flap, ch 1, sc in same st as joining and in next 32 (35) sts—33 (36) sc.

Rows 2–5 (7) Ch 1, turn; sc in each st across. Do not fasten off.

RIGHT EARFLAP (BOTH SIZES)

Rows 1–8 (9) With B, work same as Rows 1–8 (9) of Exterior Right Earflap.

Row 9 (10) Ch 1, turn; sc in each st across—4 (6) sc. Fasten off.

LEFT EARFLAP (BOTH SIZES)

Row 1 With wrong side facing and top of hat facing downward, sk next 17 (16) sts on last row of Interior Back Flap after last st worked on Row 1 of Interior Right Earflap, join B with sl st in next st, ch 1, sc in same st as joining and in next 7 (9) sts—8 (10) sc.

Rows 2–9 (10) Work same as Rows 2–9 (10) on Interior Right Earflap.

Joining

With right side facing and top of hat facing downward, working through both layers of hat exterior and lining, matching sts, join B with sl st in any st along bottom edge of hat, ch 1, sc in same st as joining and in each st around entire bottom edge of flaps and unworked sc between flaps, joining lining to exterior of hat; join with sl st in first sc. Fasten off.

FINISHING

Weave in ends. ■

EXTERIOR HAT RNDS 1–11 (LARGE)

EXTERIOR HAT RNDS 1–9 (SMALL)

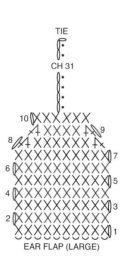

EAR FLAP (LARGE)

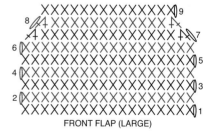

FRONT FLAP (LARGE)

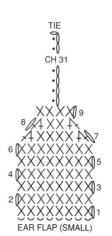

EAR FLAP (SMALL)

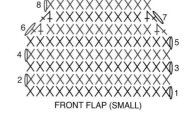

FRONT FLAP (SMALL)

Crafty Headband

MATERIALS

Yarn 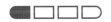 4

RED HEART *With Love*, 7oz/198g balls, each approx 370yd/338m (recycled cotton/acrylic)
• 1 ball #1303 Aran (A)

Hook
• Size H/8 (5mm) crochet hook *or size to obtain gauge*

Notions
• Embroidery floss (to match yarn color)
• Clear craft glue (optional)
• Yarn needle

SMALL CIRCLE

MEDIUM CIRCLE

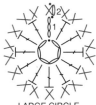
LARGE CIRCLE

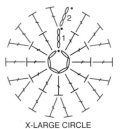
X-LARGE CIRCLE

FINISHED MEASUREMENTS
Approx 4¾"/12cm wide (at widest point) x 16½"/42cm long (plus ties)

GAUGE
Medium circle = 1½"/4cm diameter.
Take time to check gauge.

HEADBAND
Medium Circle (Make 12)
Ch 6, join with sl st to form a ring.
Rnd 1 (RS) Ch 3 (counts as dc), 11 dc in ring; join with sl st in 3rd ch of beginning ch-3—12 dc. Fasten off.

Small Circle (Make 12)
Ch 6, join with sl st to form a ring.
Rnd 1 (RS) Ch 2 (counts as hdc), 6 hdc in ring; join with sl st in 2nd ch of beginning ch-2—7 hdc. Fasten off.

Large Circle (Make 12)
Ch 6, join with sl st to form a ring.
Rnd 1 Work same as Round 1 of Medium Circle. Do not fasten off.
Rnd 2 Ch 1, sc in same ch as joining, 2 sc in next dc; *sc in next dc, 2 sc in next dc; repeat from * around; join with sl st in first sc—18 sc. Fasten off.

X-Large Circle (Make 12)
Ch 6, join with sl st to form a ring.
Rnd 1 Work same as Round 1 of Medium Circle. Do not fasten off.
Rnd 2 Ch 3 (counts as dc), dc in same ch as joining, dc in next dc; *2 dc in next dc, dc in next dc; repeat from * around; join with sl st in 3rd ch of beginning ch-3—18 dc. Fasten off.

ASSEMBLY
With right sides facing, arrange 11 Medium Circles in a line. Join edges of circles tog with embroidery floss. With right sides facing, arrange Large, X-Large and Small Circles above and below joined Medium Circles as shown in photo, or as desired. Join edges of circles tog with embroidery floss.

TIES
Join yarn with sl st at outer edge of last joined Medium Circle at end of Headband, ch 25, sc in 2nd ch from hook and in each remaining ch across; join with sl st in same st as joining—24 sc. Fasten off. Repeat at outer edge of first joined Medium Circle at other end of Headband.

FINISHING
Weave in all ends. Glue ends with craft glue, if necessary or desired. ■

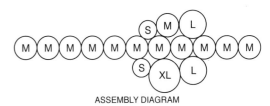
ASSEMBLY DIAGRAM

Bright Gift Ideas

Rose Callahan

MATERIALS

Yarn (3)

RED HEART *With Love*, 7oz/198g balls, each approx 370yds/338m (acrylic)

1 ball each:
- #1502 Iced Aqua (A)
- #1909 Holly Berry (B)

Note Colors listed are for the blue hat with red trim and the red scarf with blue trim. Choose whichever colors you like—we've shown a myriad of possibilities for inspiration!

Hook
- Size I/9 (5.5mm) crochet hook *or size to obtain gauges*

Notions
- Stitch marker
- Yarn needle

FINISHED MEASUREMENTS

Scarf Approx 6½"/16.5cm wide x 52"/132cm long (or desired length)
Hat Approx 19½"/50cm circumference

GAUGES

Scarf 14 sts and 11 rows in pattern = 4"/10cm
Hat Rounds 1–5 = 4"/10cm diameter
Take time to check gauges.

SCARF

With B (or color of choice), ch 23.
Row 1 (right side) Sc in 2nd ch from hook, dc in next ch; [sc in next ch, dc in next ch] 10 times—22 sts.
Row 2 Ch 1, turn; sc in first dc, dc in next sc, [sc in next dc, dc in next sc] 10 times. Repeat row 2 until you have used up one ball of yarn, scarf is approx 52"/132cm long, or to desired length. Fasten off.

Edging
With right side facing, join A (or color of choice) with sl st in first st on last row, ch 1, sc in same st as joining, sc in each st and row around, working 2 sc in edge of each dc and 1 sc in edge of each sc on side edges and 3 sc in each corner; join with sl st in first sc. Fasten off.

FINISHING

Weave in all ends.

HAT

With A or choice of color, ch 4; join with sl st to form a ring.
Round 1 (right side) Ch 1, 8 hdc in ring; join with sl st in first hdc—8 hdc.

Round 2 Ch 1, 2 hdc in same hdc as joining and in each hdc around; join—16 hdc.

Round 3 Ch 1; *hdc in next st, 2 hdc in next; repeat from * around, working last 2 hdc in joining sl st; join—24 hdc.

Round 4 Ch 1; *hdc in next 2 sts, 2 hdc in next; repeat from * around, working last 2 hdc in joining sl st; join—32 hdc.

Round 5 Ch 1; *hdc in next 3 sts, 2 hdc in next; repeat from * around, working last 2 hdc in joining sl st; join—40 hdc.

Round 6 Ch 1; *hdc in next 4 sts, 2 hdc in next; repeat from * around, working last 2 hdc in joining sl st; join—48 hdc.

Round 7 Ch 1; *hdc in next 5 sts, 2 hdc in next; repeat from * around, working last 2 hdc in joining sl st; join—56 hdc.

Round 8 Ch 1; *hdc in next 6 sts, 2 hdc in next; repeat from * around, working last 2 hdc in joining sl st; join—64 hdc.

Round 9 Ch 1; *hdc in next 15 sts, 2 hdc in next; repeat from * around, working last 2 hdc in joining sl st; do not join—68 hdc.

Round 10 Hdc in next st and in each st around. Do not join. Place a marker in last st and move up to last st in each round as work progresses.

Rounds 11–32 Repeat Round 10, 22 more times, or to desired length.

Round 33 Sc in each st around; join with sl st in first sc. Fasten off.

Edging (optional)

With wrong side facing, join B with sl st in any sc on Round 33, ch 1, sc in same sc as joining and in each sc around; join with sl st in first sc. Fasten off.

FINISHING

Weave in ends. Turn up bottom edge for brim. ∎

Stitch Diagrams

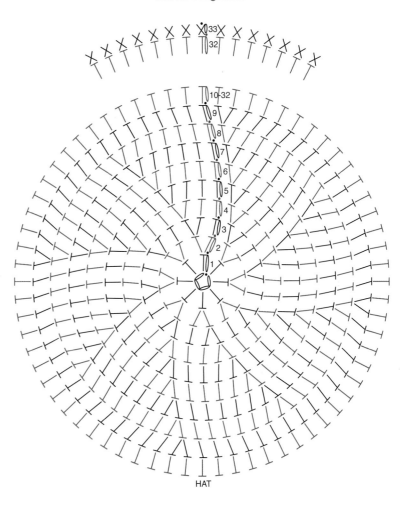

HAT

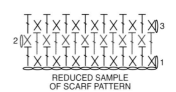

REDUCED SAMPLE
OF SCARF PATTERN

MATERIALS

Yarn 🎨
RED HEART *Light & Lofty*,
6oz/170g skeins, each approx
140yd/128m (acrylic)
• 1 skein #9112 Nightline

Hook
• Size N/15 (10mm) crochet
hook *or size to obtain gauge*

Notions
• Yarn needle

STITCH GLOSSARY

Adjustable Ring Wrap yarn
around index finger, forming a
ring. Remove ring from finger and
hold working yarn behind ring.
Insert hook into ring, yarn over
and draw a loop through
the ring. Work Round 1 in ring,
then pull tail to cinch ring closed.

Front Post Double Crochet
Yarn over, insert hook from front
to back to front around post of
specified stitch, yarn over and
draw up a loop [yarn over and
draw through 2 loops on hook]
twice.

Chunky Cap

FINISHED MEASUREMENTS
Circumference Approx 23"/58cm

GAUGE
Rounds 1–3 = 6½"/17cm diameter
Take time to check gauge.

BERET
Starting at center of crown, chain 4, join with slip stitch to form a ring (or use adjustable ring method).

Round 1 Chain 3 (counts as double crochet now and throughout), work 11 double crochets in ring—12 double crochet. Join with slip stitch in 3rd chain of beginning chain-3.

Round 2 Chain 3; *Front post double crochet around next double crochet**; 2 double crochet in next double crochet; repeat from * around, ending last repeat at **; double crochet in same chain as joining—6 front post double crochets and 12 double crochets. Join.

Round 3 Chain 3; *front post double crochet around next front post double crochet**; 2 double crochets in each of next 2 double crochets; repeat from * around, ending last repeat at **; 2 double crochets in next double crochet, double crochet in same chain as joining—6 front post double crochets and 24 double crochets. Join.

Round 4 Chain 3; *front post double crochet around next front post double crochet, 2 double crochets in next double crochet, double crochet in each of next 2 double crochets**; 2 double crochets in next double crochet; repeat from * around, ending last repeat at **; double crochet in same chain as joining—6 front post double crochets and 36 double crochets. Join.

Round 5 Working in back loops only, chain 1, single crochet in same chain as joining, single crochet in each front post double crochet and double crochet around—42 single crochet. Join with slip stitch in first single crochet.

Round 6 Chain 3, double crochet in next

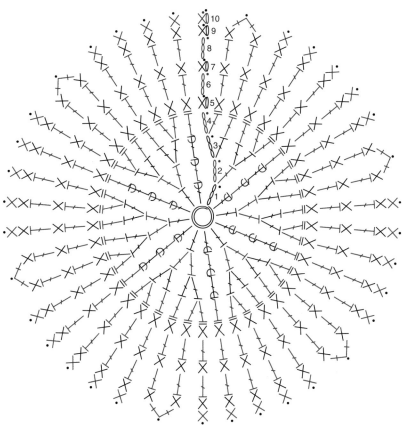

Stitch Diagram

single crochet and in each single crochet around—42 double crochets. Join with slip stitch in 3rd chain of beginning chain-3.

Round 7 Chain 1, single crochet in same chain as joining, single crochet in each double crochet around—42 single crochet. Join with slip stitch in first single crochet.

Rounds 8 and 9 Repeat Rounds 6 and 7.

Round 10 Ch 1, single crochet in first 5 single crochets, single crochet 2 together; *single crochet in next 5 single crochets, single crochet 2 together; repeat from * around—36 single crochets. Join with slip stitch in first single crochet.

Round 11 Slip stitch loosely in next single crochet and in each single crochet around. Join with slip stitch in joining slip stitch. Fasten off.

FINISHING
Weave in ends. ■

Rose Callahan

Scarves 4 Ways

MATERIALS

Yarn

Scarf 1 (5)
RED HEART *Boutique Swirl*, 3oz/85g balls, each approx 106yd/97m (polyester/acrylic/new wool/alpaca)
• 3 balls #9328 Prism (A)

Scarf 2 (4)
RED HEART *Boutique Magical*, 3½oz/100g balls, each approx 190yd/174m (acrylic/wool/other)
• 4 balls #1012 Top Hat (B)

Scarf 3 (6)
RED HEART *Light & Lofty*, 6oz/170g balls, each approx 140yd/128m (acrylic)
• 1 skein #9316 Puff (C)
• 1 skein #9632 Pine (D)

Scarf 4 (4)
RED HEART *Super Saver*, 7oz/198g balls, each approx 364yd/333m (acrylic)
• 1 skein #964 Primary (E)
RED HEART *Sport*, 2.5oz/70g skeins, each approx 172yd/157m (acrylic)
• 1 skein #0687 Paddy Green (F)
• 1 skein #0912 Cherry Red (G)

Hooks

• **Scarf 1** Size L/11 (8mm) crochet hook
• **Scarves 2 and 4** Size K/10½ (6.5mm) crochet hook
• **Scarf 3** Size P/15mm crochet hook
or size to obtain gauges

Notions

• Yarn needle

STITCH GLOSSARY

Mesh pattern stitch

Pat Row 1 Ch 2, sc in 2nd ch from hook—1 sc. Ch 1, turn.

Pat Row 2 [Sc, ch 1, sc] in first sc—2 sc. Ch 1, turn.

Pat Row 3 Sc in first sc, ch 1, sc in next ch-1 sp, ch 1, sc in last sc—3 sc. Ch 1, turn.

Pat Row 4 Sc in first sc; *ch 1, sc in next ch-1 sp; repeat from * across, ending with ch 1, sc in last sc—one more sc than last row. Ch 1, turn.

Pat Row 5 Sk first sc, sc in next ch-1 sp; *ch 1, sc in next ch-1 sp; repeat from * across, ending with ch 1, sc in last sc. Ch 1, turn.

Pat Row 6 Sk first sc, sc in next ch-1 sp; *ch 1, sc in next ch-1 sp; repeat from * across to last ch-1 sp; ch 1, sc2tog in last ch-1 sp and last sc—one less sc than last row. Ch 1, turn.

Pat Row 7 Sk first sc, sc2tog in rem ch-1 sp and last sc—1 sc.

FINISHED MEASUREMENTS

Scarf 1 Approx 7"/18cm x 71"/180.5cm
Scarf 2 Approx 12"/30.5cm x 80"/203cm
Scarf 3 Approx 9"/23cm x 61"/155cm
Scarf 4 Approx 6"/15cm x 63"/160cm

GAUGES

Scarf 1 In mesh pat, 5 sc and 4 ch-1 sps = 3½"/9cm; 9 rows = 4"/10cm
Scarf 2 In mesh pat, 7 sc and 6 ch-1 sps = 4"/10cm; 12 rows = 4"/10cm
Scarf 3 In mesh pat, 9 sc and 8 ch-1 sps = 9"/23cm, 9 rows = 5"/12.5cm
Scarf 4 With E, bias square = 6"/15cm square; with F or G in mesh pat, 10 sc and 9 ch-1 sps = 6"/15cm; 7 rows = 2"/5cm
Gauge is not critical for these scarves.
Note Mesh fabric will lengthen and narrow when worn.

SCARF 1

Use A and Size L/11 (8mm) crochet hook.
Rows 1–10 Work Pat Rows 1-4, then repeat Pat Row 4 six times more, or until desired width of scarf—10 sc and 9 ch-1 sps at end of Row 10.
Rows 11–151 Work Pat Row 5 until scarf measures approx 67"/170cm, or until desired length of scarf before working the ending point.

Rows 152–160 Work Pat Row 6 eight times, then work pat row 7 once. Fasten off.

FINISHING
Weave in all ends.

SCARF 2

Use B and Size K/10½ (6.5mm) crochet hook.
Rows 1–21 Work Pat Rows 1–4, then repeat Pat Row 4 seventeen times more, or until desired width of scarf—21 sc and 20 chs at end of Row 21.
Rows 22–220 Work Pat Row 5 until scarf measures approx 73"/185.5cm, or until desired length of scarf before working the ending point.
Rows 221–240 Work Pat Row 6 nineteen times, then work Pat Row 7 once. Fasten off.

FINISHING
Weave in all ends.

SCARF 3

With C and Size P/15mm crochet hook, ch 18.
Row 1 Sc in 2nd ch from hook, [ch 1, sk next ch, sc in next ch] 8 times—9 sc and 8 ch-1 sps. Ch 1, turn.
Rows 2–5 Work Pat Row 5 four times, changing to D in last sc. Drop and cut C.

Scarves 4 Ways

Rows 6–40 Beginning with D, then alternating bet C and D, make 35-row striping sequence shown below, working in pat row 5. Each number in striping sequence indicates number of rows worked in each color. Change to opposite color in last st on last row of each striped section. Striping sequence [1, 5, 2, 4, 3, 3, 4, 2, 5, 1, 5]

Rows 41–75 Repeat striping sequence, now beginning with C.

Rows 76–110 Repeat striping sequence once more, now beginning with D. Fasten off.

FINISHING
Weave in all ends.

SCARF 4
Use E, F and G and Size K/10½ (6.5mm) crochet hook.

NOTE
There is no obvious right side or wrong side on squares or bands.

Bias Square (Make 7)
Each motif begins with a bias square in E starting and ending at points, made by increase rows, then decrease rows.

Rows 1–13 With E, work Pat Rows 1–4, then repeat Pat Row 4 nine times more—13 sc and 12 ch-1 sps.

Row 14 Work Pat Row 5.

Rows 15–26 Work Pat Row 6 eleven times, then work Pat Row 7 once. Fasten off.

Color Bands
Each Bias Square has 13 sc row edges along each side. Make a band of F in mesh stitch on one side of square, then a band of G on opposite side, easing stitches to fit.

F-Band
From fastened off last sc of bias square, rotate to work from corner to corner across edge of 13 rows along one side.

Row 1 Join F with sl st in left edge of last row of bias square, ch 1, sc in edge of same row, ch 1, sc in edge of next row, ch 1; *sk next row, [sc in edge of next row, ch 1] 3 times; repeat from * once; sk next row, sc in edge of next row, ch 1, sc in edge of last row—10 sc and 9 ch-1 sps. Ch 1, turn.

Rows 2–7 Work Pat Row 5 six times. Fasten off, leaving long tail for sewing.

G-Band
From beginning sc of same Bias Square, work from corner to corner across edge of 13 rows along side opposite F Band.

Row 1 Join G with sl st in edge of first row, work in same manner as F Band Row 1—10 sc and 9 ch-1 sps.

Rows 2–4 Work Pat Row 5 three times. Fasten off.

Work F and G Bands on other bias squares in same manner.

ASSEMBLY
Use photograph as a guide. Arrange motifs end to end, with F Band meeting G Band. Flip motifs as needed to alternate diagonal stripes of bias squares. Using long tail of F and yarn needle, holding edges of F and G Bands together, matching stitches, whip-stitch in each sc and ch-1 sp through both thicknesses. Fasten off. Join rest of motifs in same manner.

FINISHING
Weave in all ends. ■

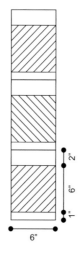

Raspberry Beret

MATERIALS

Yarn 🧶 4

RED HEART *Soft*, 5oz/140g skeins, each approx 256yd/234m (acrylic)
• 1 skein #4608 Wine

Hook

• Size J/10 (6mm) crochet hook *or size to obtain gauge*

Notions

• Yarn needle

STITCH GLOSSARY

beginning bobble Ch 3; [yarn over, insert hook in same st as joining, yarn over and draw up a loop, yarn over and draw through 2 loops on hook] 2 times; yarn over and draw through all 3 loops on hook.

bobble *Yarn over, insert hook in indicated st, yarn over and draw up a loop, yarn over and draw through 2 loops on hook; repeat from * 2 more times in same st; yarn over and draw through all 4 loops on hook.

dc4tog (double crochet 4 stitches together) [Yarn over, insert hook in next st, yarn over and draw up a loop, yarn over and draw through 2 loops on hook] 4 times; yarn over and draw through all 5 loops on hook.

dc2tog (double crochet 2 stitches together) [Yarn over, insert hook in next st, yarn over and draw up a loop, yarn over and draw through 2 loops on hook] 2 times; yarn over and draw through all 3 loops on hook.

SPECIAL TECHNIQUE

Adjustable ring method Holding the yarn a few inches from the end, wrap around your finger. Do not remove wrap from finger, insert hook into the wrap and draw up a loop of working yarn. Chain one to secure the loop, and remove ring from finger. Work stitches of first round in the ring. Pull gently, but firmly, on tail to tighten ring.

FINISHED MEASUREMENTS

Circumference at brim 18"/45.5cm
Stretches to fit up to 21"/53cm head.

GAUGE

Rounds 1–3 = 3¼"/8.5cm diameter
Take time to check gauge.

BERET

Starting at crown, make an adjustable ring.

Round 1 Work 8 sc in ring; join with sl st in first sc—8 sc.

Round 2 Work beginning bobble, ch 2, *bobble in next sc, ch 2; repeat from * around, join with sl st in top of beginning bobble—8 bobbles and 8 ch-2 sps.

Round 3 Ch 5 (counts as dc and ch-2 sp), *dc in next ch-2 sp, ch 2**, dc in next bobble, ch 2; repeat from * around, ending last repeat at **; join with sl st in 3rd ch of beginning ch-5—16 dc and 16 ch-2 sps.

Round 4 Ch 1, sc in same ch as joining, *ch 5, sk next ch-2 sp, sc in next dc; repeat from * around; join with ch 2, dc in first sc (counts as ch-5 sp)—16 sc and 16 ch-5 sps.

Round 5 Ch 1, sc around post of joining dc, *2 dc in next sc, sc in next ch-5 sp**, ch 5, sk next sc, sc in next ch-5 sp; repeat from * around, ending last repeat at **; join with ch 2, sk next sc, dc in first sc (counts as ch-5 sp)—16 dc, 16 sc and 8 ch-5 sps.

Round 6 Ch 1, sc around post of joining dc, *ch 5, dc4tog in next 4 sts (sc, 2 dc, sc), ch 5**, sc in next ch-5 sp; repeat from * around, ending last repeat at **; join with sl st in first sc—8 dc4tog, 8 sc and 16 ch-5 sps.

Round 7 Sl st in next ch, ch 3 (counts as dc here and throughout), dc in each ch around, skipping all sc and dc4tog; join with sl st in 3rd ch of beginning ch-3—80 dc.

Round 8 Ch 3, dc in next dc, ch 1, sk next dc, dc in next 2 dc, *ch 1, sk next dc, 2 dc in next dc**, [ch 1, sk next dc, dc in next 2 dc] twice; repeat from * around, ending last repeat at **, ch 1; join with sl st in 3rd ch of beginning ch-3—60 dc and 30 ch-1 sps.

Round 9 Ch 3, dc in next dc, *[dc in next ch, dc in next 2 dc] twice, 2 dc in next ch**, dc in next 2 dc; repeat from * around, ending last repeat at **; join with sl st in 3rd ch of beginning ch-3—100 dc.

Round 10 Ch 3, dc in next 9 dc, *[dc in next 9 dc, 2 dc in next dc] 4 times**, dc in next 10 sts; repeat from * to ** once; join with sl st in 3rd ch of beginning ch-3—108 dc.

Round 11 Ch 3, dc in next dc, *ch 1, sk next dc, dc in next 2 dc; repeat from * around, ch 1, sk next dc; join with sl st in 3rd ch of beginning ch-3—72 dc and 36 ch-1 sps.

Raspberry Beret

Round 12 Ch 3, dc in next dc, dc in each ch and dc around; join with sl st in 3rd ch of beginning ch-3—108 dc.

Round 13 Ch 3, dc in next dc and in each dc around; join with sl st in 3rd ch of beginning ch-3.

Round 14 Ch 3, dc in next dc, *ch 1, sk next dc, dc2tog, ch 1, sk next dc**, dc in next 2 dc; repeat from * around, ending last repeat at **; join with sl st in 3rd ch of beginning ch-3—54 dc and 36 ch-1 sps.

Round 15 Ch 3, dc in next 6 sts (dc and chs), dc2tog, *dc in next 7 sts, dc2tog; repeat from * around; join with sl st in 3rd ch of beginning ch-3—80 dc.

Round 16 Ch 3, dc in next dc, dc2tog, *dc in next 2 dc, dc2tog; repeat from * around; join with sl st in 3rd ch of beginning ch-3—60 dc.

Round 17 Repeat Round 14—30 dc and 20 ch-1 sps.

Round 18 Ch 3, dc in next dc, dc in each ch and dc around; join with sl st in 3rd ch of beginning ch-3—50 dc.

Rounds 19–22 Ch 1, sc in same st as joining and in each st around; join with sl st in first sc—50 sc. At end of Round 22, fasten off and weave in ends. ■

Stitch Diagram

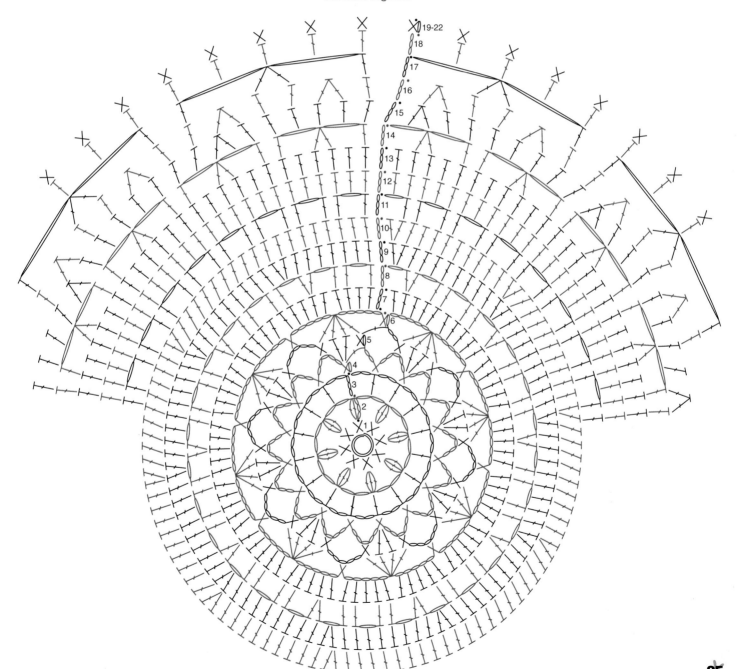

Super Soft Set

MATERIALS

Yarn

RED HEART *Soft*, 5oz/140g skeins, each approx 256yd/234m (acrylic)
• 2 skeins #9518 Teal

Hook
• Size I/9 (5.5mm) crochet hook *or size to obtain gauge*

Notions
• Stitch markers

SCARF
FINISHED MEASUREMENTS
Length Approx 61"/156cm
Width Approx 5½"/14cm

GAUGE
13 sts + 13 rows = 4"/10cm
Take time to check gauge.

NOTE
Work on one side of beginning ch and then on the other side as specified. Leave 6"/15cm ends of yarn when beginning and fastening off to tie into final fringe.

FIRST HALF
Beginning at center of scarf, ch 202.
Row 1 (right side) Sc in 2nd ch from hook and in each ch across—201 sc. Ch 1, turn.
Row 2 Work (sc, dc) in first sc; *sk next sc, (sc, dc) in next sc; repeat from * across—202 sts. Ch 1, turn.
Row 3 Sk first dc, (sc, dc) in next sc; *sk next dc, (sc, dc) in next sc; repeat from * across. Ch 1, turn.
Row 4 Repeat row 3.
Row 5 Sk first dc, sc in next sc; *ch 1, sk next dc, sc in next sc; repeat from * across—101 sc and 100 chs. Ch 1, turn.
Row 6 Sc in first sc; *sc in next ch-1 sp, sc in next sc; repeat from * across—201 sc. Ch 1, turn.

Row 7 Sc in each sc across. Ch 1, turn.
Rows 8 and 9 Repeat rows 2 and 3 once more. Fasten off.

SECOND HALF
Row 1 With right side facing, working in free lps of chs on opposite side of foundation ch, insert hook in first ch and draw up a lp, ch 1, sc in same ch, sc in next ch and in each ch across— 201 sc. Ch 1, turn.
Rows 2–9 Repeat rows 2–9 on First Half.

Fringe
Cut 65 strands of yarn, each 12"/30cm long. Space fringe evenly across each end of scarf, making one fringe in foundation ch in center and 5 fringe in each half for a total of 11 fringe on each end. Use 2 strands for fringe at beginning of foundation ch where 2 ends remain and 3 strands for all other fringe. Pull strands through end of row. Fold strands in half and tie in an overhand knot, including end from row in knot where appropriate. Trim fringe to 4"/10cm.

HAT
FINISHED MEASUREMENTS
Circumference 20"/50cm (adult medium)

GAUGE
Rounds 1–6 = 4"/10cm diameter
Take time to check gauge.

NOTES
Use size G or H hook to make a smaller hat or size J hook to make a larger hat. Do not join Rounds 1–11, but work in continuous rounds. Mark last sc on Rounds 1–11, moving marker up as you work.

HAT
Beginning at top of hat, ch 4; join with sl st to form a ring.
Round 1 (right side) Ch 1, work 8 sc in ring—8 sc.
Round 2 Work 2 sc in each sc around—16 sc.
Round 3 *Sc in next sc, 2 sc in next sc; repeat from * around—24 sc.

Round 4 *Sc in next 2 sc, 2 sc in next sc; repeat from * around—32 sc.
Round 5 *Work 2 sc in next sc, sc in next 3 sc; repeat from * around—40 sc.
Round 6 *Sc in next 4 sc, 2 sc in next sc; repeat from * around—48 sc.
Rounds 7 and 8 Sc in each sc around.
Round 9 *Sc in next 5 sc, 2 sc in next sc; repeat from * around—56 sc.
Round 10 Sc in each sc around.
Round 11 *Work 2 sc in next sc, sc in next 6 sc; repeat from * around—64 sc.
Round 12 Sc in each sc around; join with sl st in first sc. Ch 1, turn.
Round 13 (wrong side) Work (sc, dc) in first sc, sk next sc; *(sc, dc) in next sc, sk next sc; repeat from * around; join as before—64 sts. Ch 1, turn.
Round 14 (right side) Sk first dc, (sc, dc) in next sc; *sk next dc, (sc, dc) in next sc; repeat from * around; join as before. Ch 1, turn.
Round 15 Repeat round 14.
Round 16 Sc in first sc, ch 1, sk next dc, *sc in next sc, ch 1; sk next dc; repeat from * around; sk last sc; join as before—32 sc and 32 ch-1 sps. Ch 1, turn.
Round 17 *Sc in next ch-1 sp, sc in next sc; repeat from * around; join as before—64 sc. Ch 1, turn.
Round 18 Sc in each sc around. Join as before. Ch 1, turn.
Rounds 19–30 Repeat Rounds 13–18 two times more.
Rounds 31–33 Repeat Rounds 13–15 once more. At end of Round 33, do not ch 1. Fasten off.

FINISHING
Weave in all ends. Turn up last 7 rows to form cuff. ■

Stitch Diagram

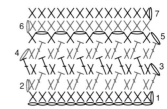

REDUCED SAMPLE OF PATTERN

27

Retro Striped Hat

MATERIALS

Yarn

RED HEART *Soft*, 5oz/140g balls, each approx 256yd/234m (acrylic)
- 1 ball #9344 Chocolate (A)
- 1 ball #9523 Dark Leaf (B)
- 1 ball #3729 Grape (C)

Hook
- Size I/9 (5.5mm) crochet hook
  or size to obtain gauge

Notions
- Small pom-pom maker, 2"/5cm diameter
- Yarn needle

STITCH GLOSSARY

Front Post double crochet Yarn over, insert hook from front to back to front around post of indicated stitch; yarn over and draw up loop, [yarn over and draw through 2 loops on hook] twice.

FINISHED MEASUREMENTS
Circumference at lower edge
Approx 24"/61cm

GAUGE
13 stitches and 8 rows = 4"/10cm in double crochet using size I/9 (5.5mm) crochet hook.
Take time to check gauge.

NOTE
Change color in the join of a round. Insert hook in first stitch of the round, yarn over with the new color and draw through all loops on hook. Cut and weave in the old color, or carry loosely up the inside of the hat.

HAT

With A, make an adjustable ring as follows: Wrap yarn around index finger, forming a ring, remove ring from finger and hold working yarn behind ring. Insert hook into ring, yarn over and draw a loop through the ring. Work Round 1 in ring, then pull tail to cinch ring closed.

Round 1 Chain 3 (counts as first double crochet here and throughout), work 9 more double crochet in ring; join with slip stitch in top of beginning ch—10 double crochet

Round 2 Chain 3, double crochet in same stitch as join (increase made), 2 double crochet in each stitch around; join with slip stitch in top of beginning chain— 20 double crochet.

Round 3 Chain 3, double crochet in same stitch as join, double crochet in next stitch, [2 double crochet in next stitch, double crochet in next stitch] 9 times; join and change to C with slip stitch in top of beginning chain—30 double crochet.

Round 4 With C, chain 3, double crochet in same stitch as join, double crochet in next 2 stitches, [2 double crochet in next stitch, double crochet in next 2 stitches] 9 times; join and change to B with slip stitch in top of beginning chain—40 double crochet.

Round 5 With B, chain 1 (counts as first single crochet here and throughout), single crochet in same stitch as join, single crochet in next 3 stitches, [2 single crochet in next stitch, single crochet in next 3 stitches] 9 times; join and change to A with slip stitch in beginning chain—50 single crochet.

Round 6 With A, chain 2 (counts as first half double crochet here and throughout), half double crochet in same stitch as join, half double crochet in next 4 stitches, [2 half double crochet in next stitch, half double crochet in next 4 stitches] 9 times; join and change to B with slip stitch in top of beginning chain—60 half double crochet.

Round 7 With B, chain 3, double crochet in same stitch as join, double crochet in next 5 stitches, [2 double crochet in next stitch, double crochet in next 5 stitches] 9 times; join with slip stitch in top of beginning chain—70 double crochet.

Round 8 Chain 3, double crochet in each stitch around; join with slip stitch in top of beginning chain.

Round 9 Chain 2, half double crochet in each stitch around; join and change to C with slip stitch in top of beginning ch.

Round 10 With C, chain 2, half double crochet in each stitch around; join and change to A with slip stitch in top of beginning chain.

Round 11 With A, chain 3, double crochet in each stitch around; join and change to B with slip stitch in top of beginning chain.

Round 12 With B, chain 1, single crochet in each stitch around; join and change to C with slip stitch in beginning chain.

Round 13 With C, chain 1, single crochet in each stitch around; join and change to A with slip stitch in beginning chain.

Round 14 With A, chain 3, double crochet in each stitch around; join with slip stitch in top of beginning chain.

Round 15 Chain 3, double crochet in each stitch around; join and change to B with slip stitch in top of beginning chain.

Round 16 (front post stitch round) With B, chain 3, Front Post double crochet around beginning chain of previous round, *double crochet in next stitch, Front Post double crochet around same stitch; repeat from * around; join with slip stitch in top of beginning chain—140 stitches.

Round 17 Chain 3, skipping all Front Post double crochets of Round 16, double crochet in each double crochet around; join with slip stitch in top of beginning chain—70 double crochet.

Round 18 (front post stitch round) Ch 3, Front Post double crochet around first Front Post double crochet 2 rows below, *double crochet in next stitch, Front Post double crochet around next Front Post double crochet 2 rows below; repeat from * around; join with slip stitch in top of beginning chain—140 stitches.

Round 19 Ch 3, skipping all Front Post double crochet of Round 18, double crochet in each double crochet around; join with slip stitch in top of beginning chain—70 double crochet.

Round 20 Repeat Round 18.

Round 21 Chain 1, skipping all Front Post double crochet of previous round, slip stitch in each double crochet around; join with slip stitch in beginning chain. Fasten off.

FINISHING

Weave in all ends. With C and pompom maker, make a 2"/5cm pom-pom. Sew pom-pom to top of hat. ■

Rose Callahan

Stitch Diagrams

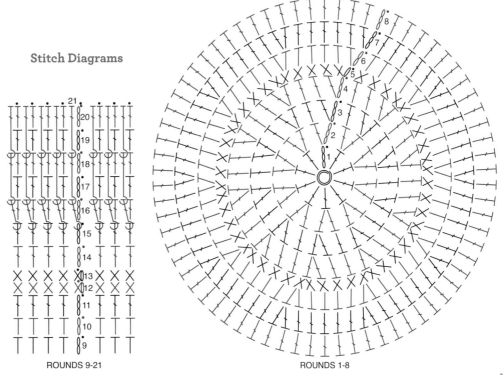

ROUNDS 9-21   ROUNDS 1-8

Sparkly Scarf

STITCH GLOSSARY

Bsl st (bead slip stitch) Remove loop from larger hook and place on smaller hook, insert hook through hole of paillette, yarn over and draw through paillette and loop on hook. Remove loop from smaller hook and place on larger hook. Gently pull on loop to tighten Bsl st. See step-by-step photos on page 32.

TIP

Try using beads or charms instead of paillettes. Just be sure the embellishment you choose has a hole large enough to accommodate the hook and yarn.

FINISHED MEASUREMENTS

Length Approx 44"/111.5cm
Width Approx 11"/28cm

GAUGE

2 pattern repeats (18 sts) and 12 rows = 4"/10cm over pattern st.
Take time to check gauge.

SCARF

With larger hook, ch 44.
Row 1 3 sc in 2nd ch from hook, *ch 6, sk next 6 ch, 3 sc in next ch; repeat from * across—6 pattern repeats.

Row 2 Ch 1, turn, 3 sc in center sc of first 3-sc group, *ch 6, sk next ch-6 sp, 3 sc in center sc of next 3-sc group; repeat from * across.
Repeat Row 2, an even number of times, until wrap measures 44"/111.5cm (or desired length). Do not fasten off.

Edging

Pivot piece to work along a long side edge.
Round 1 Working in ends of rows along edge, Bsl st, 3 sc in first row (corner), Bsl st; *sc in next row, 2 sc in next row, Bsl st; repeat from * along long side edge to last row, Bsl st, 3 sc in last row (corner), Bsl st; pivot to work in free loops along

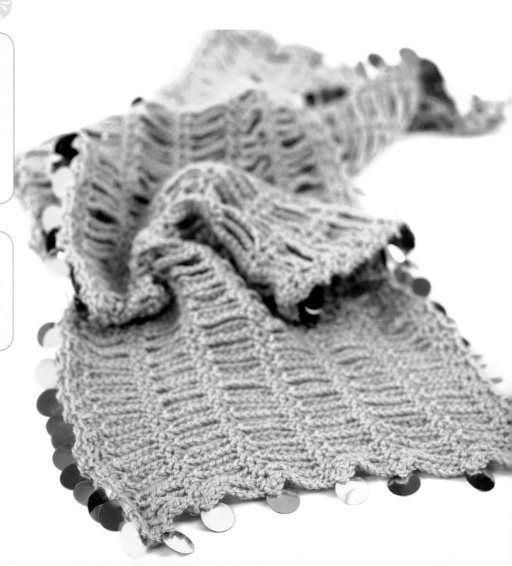

opposite side of foundation ch, 3 sc in first ch (at base of 3-sc group), Bsl st, **ch 6, sk next ch-6 sp, 3 sc in next ch (at base of 3-sc group), Bsl st; repeat from ** across foundation ch; pivot to work in ends of rows along opposite long side edge, 3 sc in first row (corner), Bsl st, ***sc in next row, 2 sc in next row, Bsl st; repeat from *** along long side edge to last row, 3 sc in last row (corner), Bsl st; pivot to work in sts of last row of scarf, sk first sc, 3 sc in next sc (center sc of 3-sc group), ****Bsl st, ch 6, sk next ch-6 sp, 3 sc in center sc of next 3-sc group; repeat from **** to end; join with sl st in first sc. Fasten off.

FINISHING

Weave in all ends. Block lightly, if desired. ■

Stitch Diagram

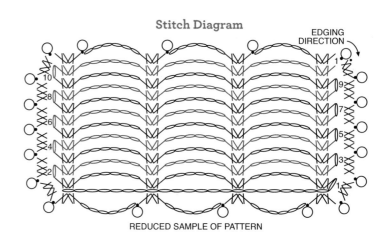

EDGING DIRECTION

REDUCED SAMPLE OF PATTERN

Attaching The Paillettes

1 After removing loop from larger hook, use smaller crochet hook (not shown) to pull loop through hole of paillette.

2 Place loop back on larger hook.

3 Pull first loop through second loop on hook to complete slip stitch.